Fashion Illustration:
Figure Drawing

p

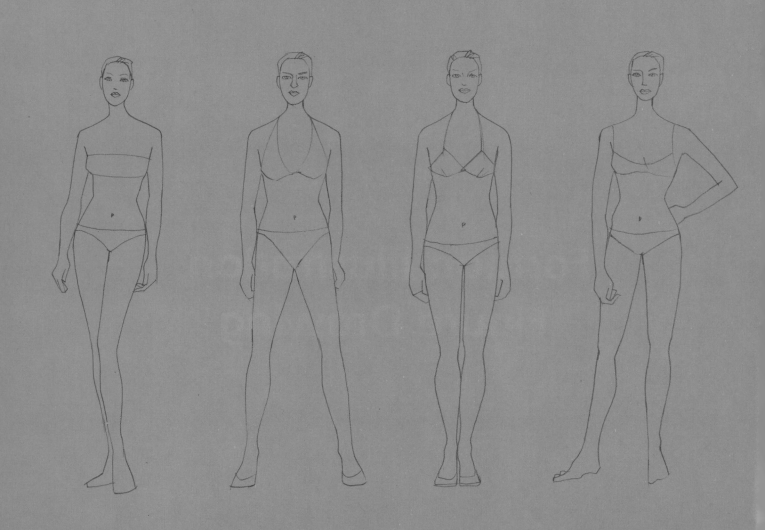

Fashion Illustration:
Figure Drawing

This is a Parragon Publishing book

Copyright © 2007 Parragon Books Ltd

Parragon Books Ltd
Queen Street House
4 Queen Street
Bath BA1 1HE, UK

Produced by Loft
Illustrations: Maite Lafuente
Text: Aitana Lleonart
Editorial coordinator: Catherine Collin
Art director: Mireia Casanovas Soley
Layout: Emma Termes Parera

US edition produced by Cambridge Publishing Management Ltd
Translator: Leslie Ray
Copy-editor: Sandra Stafford

ISBN: 978-1-4054-9431-1 (with jacket)
ISBN: 978-1-4075-0116-1 (without jacket)

Printed in China

Contents

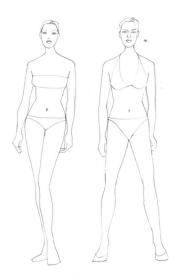

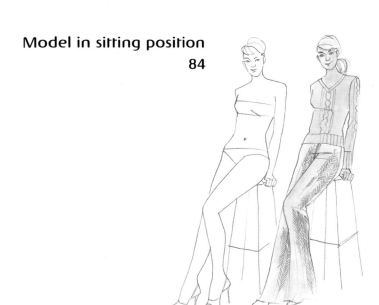

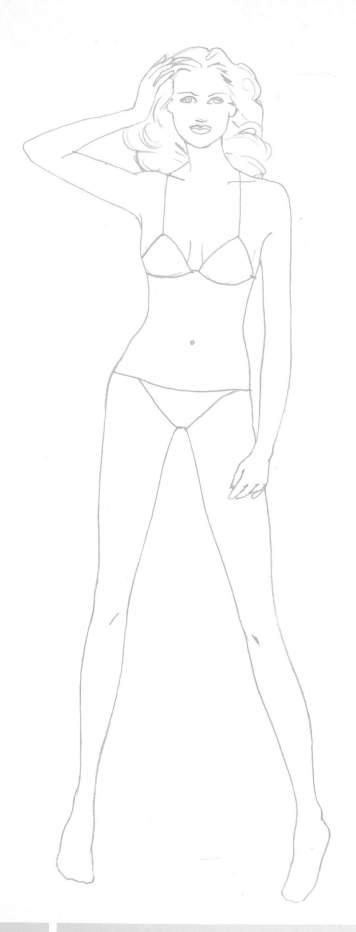

INTRODUCTION: FROM TECHNIQUE TO PERSONAL STYLE

Creativity and artistic talent are sometimes stifled by the lack of the necessary technical knowledge required to express them. This book is intended to be a tool to help you to master the key elements in the illustration of fashion sketches to enable you to visualize the ideas and projects that spring from your imagination.

To get to know the anatomical proportions, how to displace the weight of the body in the various poses, or how to make turning movements look natural—these are just some of the techniques that need to be learned if, later on, you want to develop your own style, to create your own fashion sketches, to stylize them or change their shapes, always giving free rein to your creativity.

Throughout the history of the sketch, strongly associated with fashion since the mid-nineteenth century as a tool for visualizing concepts, artists have first had to learn to express themselves in the style of the old school, the Realist school, to then evolve toward more abstract ideas. They have all had to gain an understanding of technique and the rules of proportion before devoting themselves to more avant-garde movements. This is the case of such geniuses in painting as Van Gogh and Picasso, whose early works were Realist in nature, but who subsequently immersed themselves in Neo-Impressionism and Cubism respectively. Yet it must not be forgotten that the technique they learned underpinned all their creations, even if ultimately it only served to enable them to break completely with its tenets.

To get ahead in the world of fashion illustration, the first step is to have a good grasp of drawing from life. This can only be achieved through practice: learning how to represent the various movements, how to reflect the proportions of the parts of the body, and discover the secret to achieving the naturalness necessary to give fashion sketches a sensation of realism. Once this has been achieved, it is time to apply the more creative part: that of the clothing. The volumes and hang of the cloth, clinging to the body or loose; seams, sleeves, and collars all have infinite variations. With the help of this book, you will be able to apply them to your sketches in a way that is correct and consistent with each pose.

This book will help you to put on paper all those ideas that spring to mind only to disappear because you have been unable to represent how you imagined them. The many examples of poses that illustrate the pages of this book make it a perfect template, an indispensable volume for your desktop. It will enable you to sketch a wide variety of poses and gestures by observing and reproducing the numerous figures included here. You will then be able to go on to focus on the clothing without any restrictions on your creativity.

If we look back on the history of the creative arts, we find a personality whose talent in sketching opened the doors of the world of fashion to him: Paul Poiret. His drawing skills enabled him to find employment in the workshop of Jacques Doucet, a famous couturier of the period; a few years later Poiret, now a celebrity, dressed the most renowned and admired personalities in the Parisian society of the time.

Over the years many other designers and couturiers have left their mark thanks to their creations; these include Jeanne Paquin, the genuine pioneer of the fashion parade as spectacle, Lanvin, Chanel, Calvin Klein, and Jean Paul Gaultier among others. All initially expressed their talent through their own particular styles of fashion sketches, which they colored or printed using the most diverse techniques (colored pencils, watercolors, felt-tip pens, wax crayons, etc.).

In short, the intention of this book is to provide readers with the necessary tools to recreate their ideas as faithfully as possible in illustrations and, in turn, to encourage them to find their own style. Today fashion illustrations are not just a means of visual representation but are understood as art forms in their own right, opening up new perspectives in the world of design and creativity that must not be allowed to slip away.

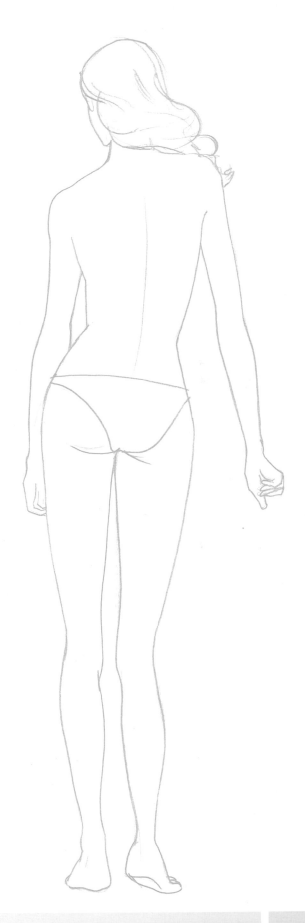

Body and proportions

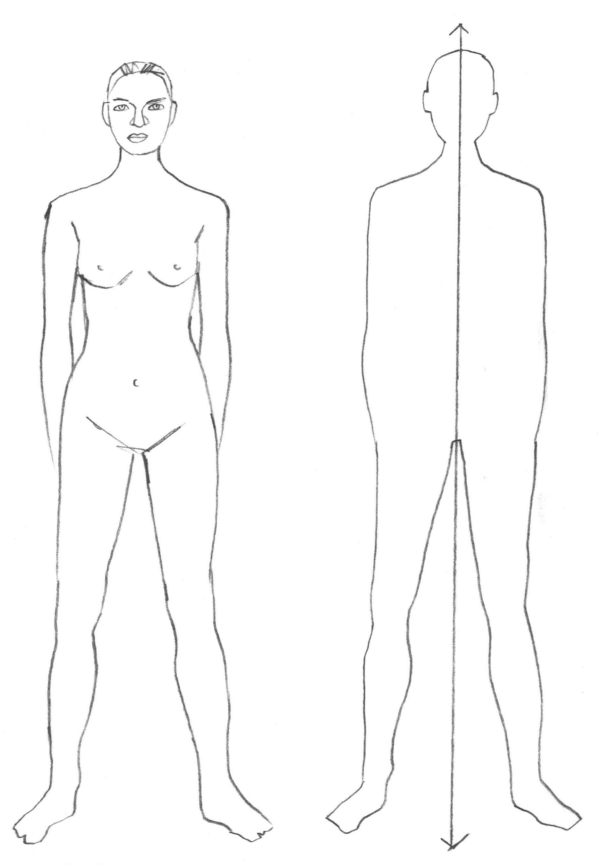

The balance of the figure is the most important factor when drawing a standing pose. The image must be very upright, otherwise it may give the impression that the body is about to fall over.

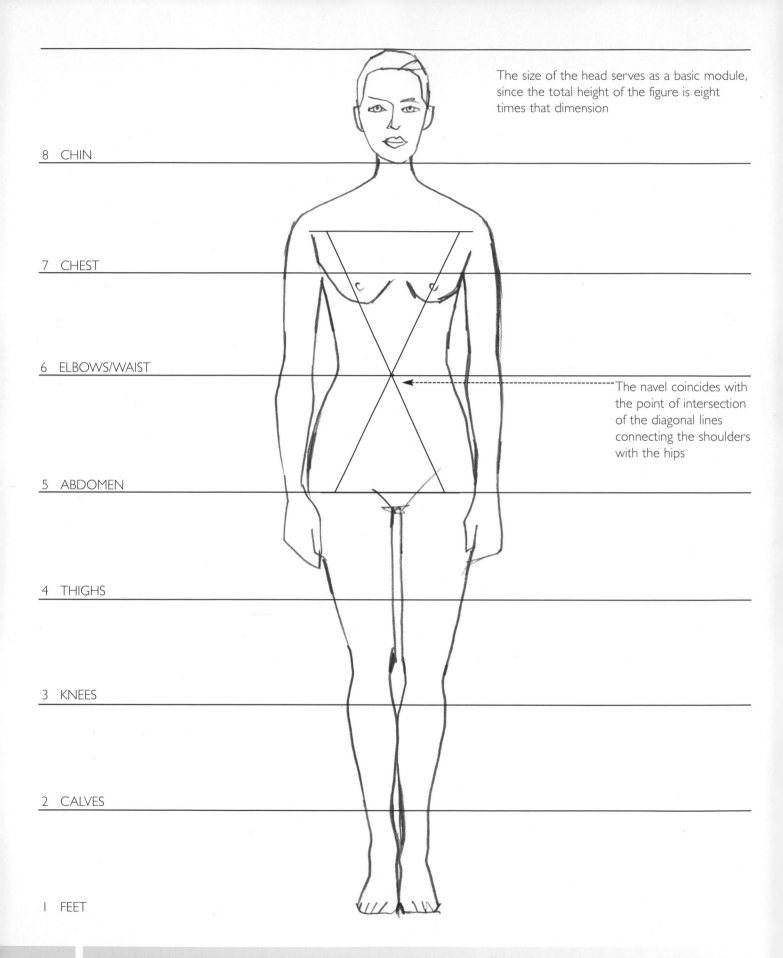

The size of the head serves as a basic module, since the total height of the figure is eight times that dimension

8 CHIN

7 CHEST

6 ELBOWS/WAIST

The navel coincides with the point of intersection of the diagonal lines connecting the shoulders with the hips

5 ABDOMEN

4 THIGHS

3 KNEES

2 CALVES

I FEET

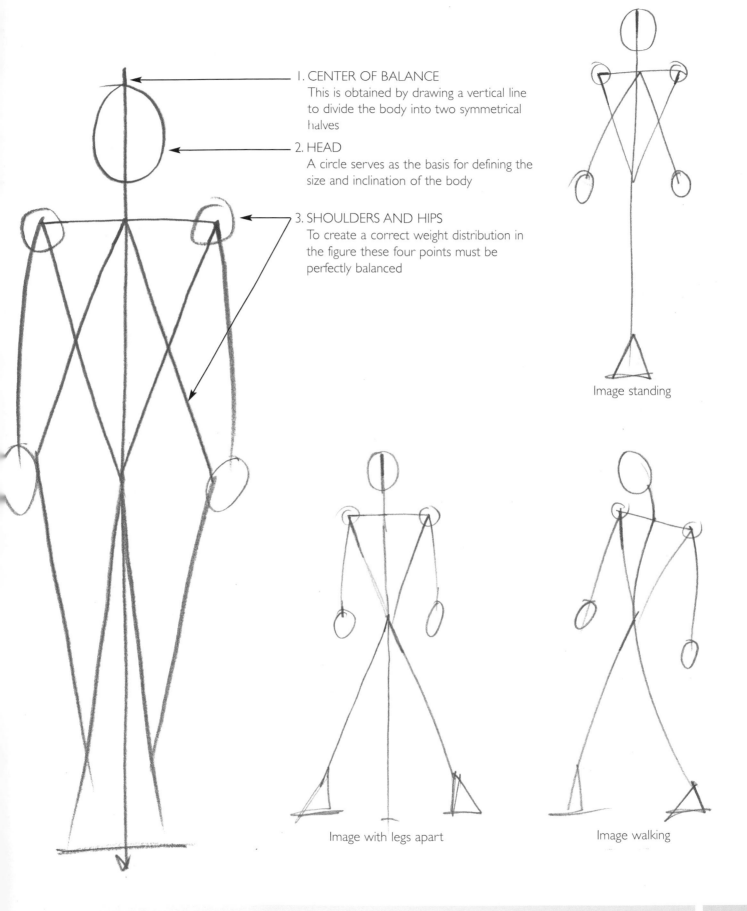

1. CENTER OF BALANCE
   This is obtained by drawing a vertical line to divide the body into two symmetrical halves

2. HEAD
   A circle serves as the basis for defining the size and inclination of the body

3. SHOULDERS AND HIPS
   To create a correct weight distribution in the figure these four points must be perfectly balanced

Image standing

Image with legs apart

Image walking

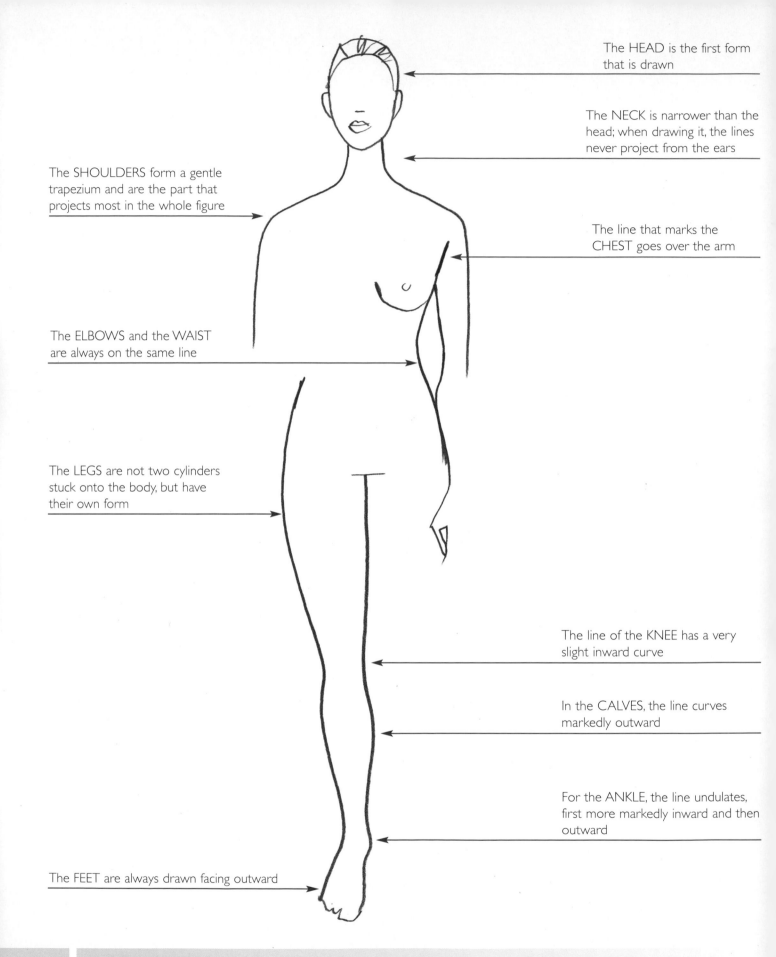

The HEAD is the first form
that is drawn

The NECK is narrower than the
head; when drawing it, the lines
never project from the ears

The SHOULDERS form a gentle
trapezium and are the part that
projects most in the whole figure

The line that marks the
CHEST goes over the arm

The ELBOWS and the WAIST
are always on the same line

The LEGS are not two cylinders
stuck onto the body, but have
their own form

The line of the KNEE has a very
slight inward curve

In the CALVES, the line curves
markedly outward

For the ANKLE, the line undulates,
first more markedly inward and then
outward

The FEET are always drawn facing outward

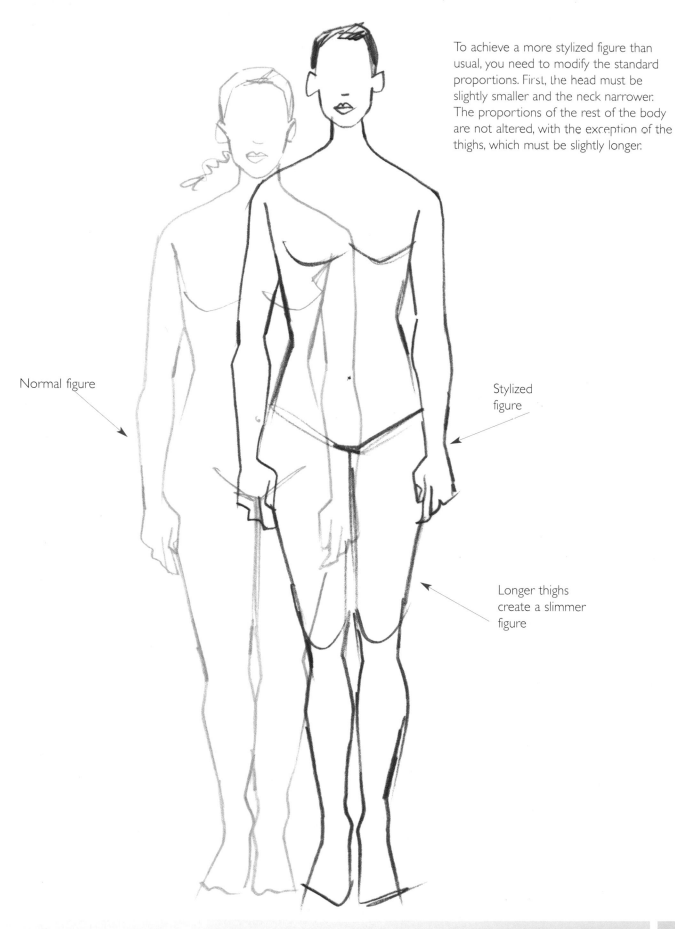

To achieve a more stylized figure than usual, you need to modify the standard proportions. First, the head must be slightly smaller and the neck narrower. The proportions of the rest of the body are not altered, with the exception of the thighs, which must be slightly longer.

Normal figure

Stylized figure

Longer thighs create a slimmer figure

Fashion sketches

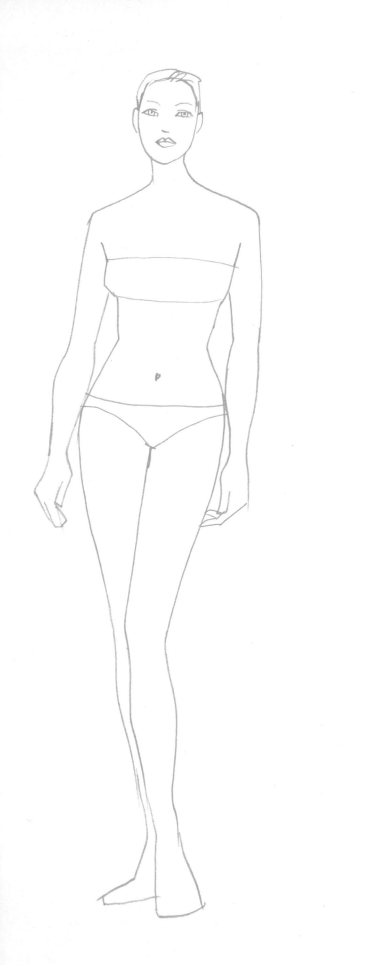
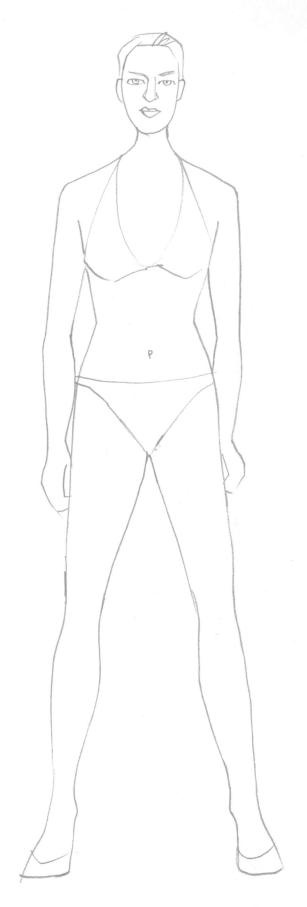

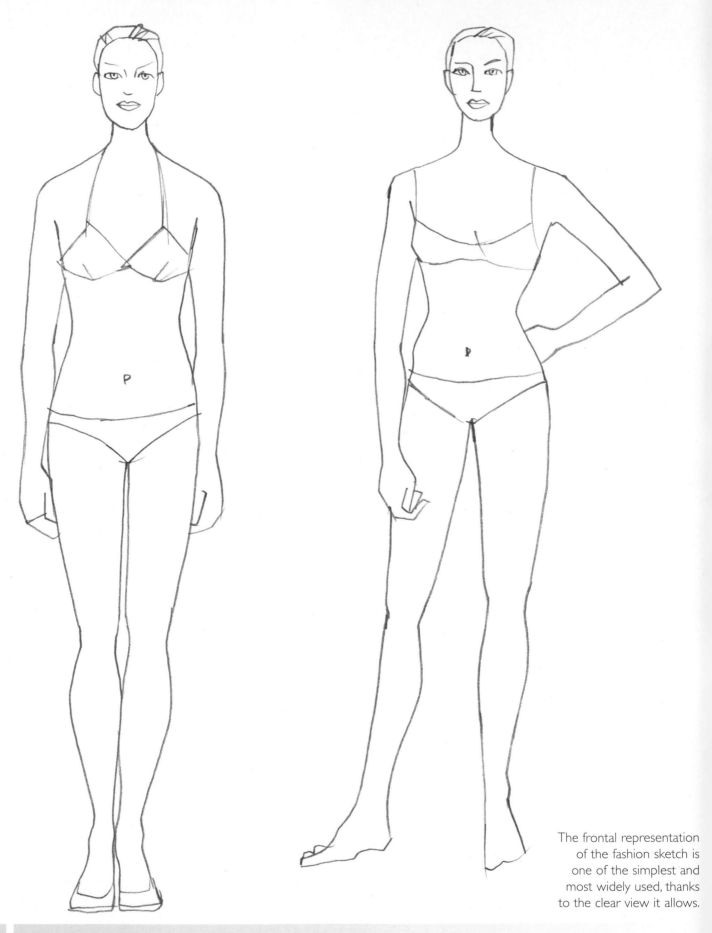

The frontal representation of the fashion sketch is one of the simplest and most widely used, thanks to the clear view it allows.

With this pose you can show tops and upper clothing combined with long pants, shorts, Capri shorts or any model that fits the leg closely.

Certain positions of the legs and turning positions allow you to show the clothing in movement.

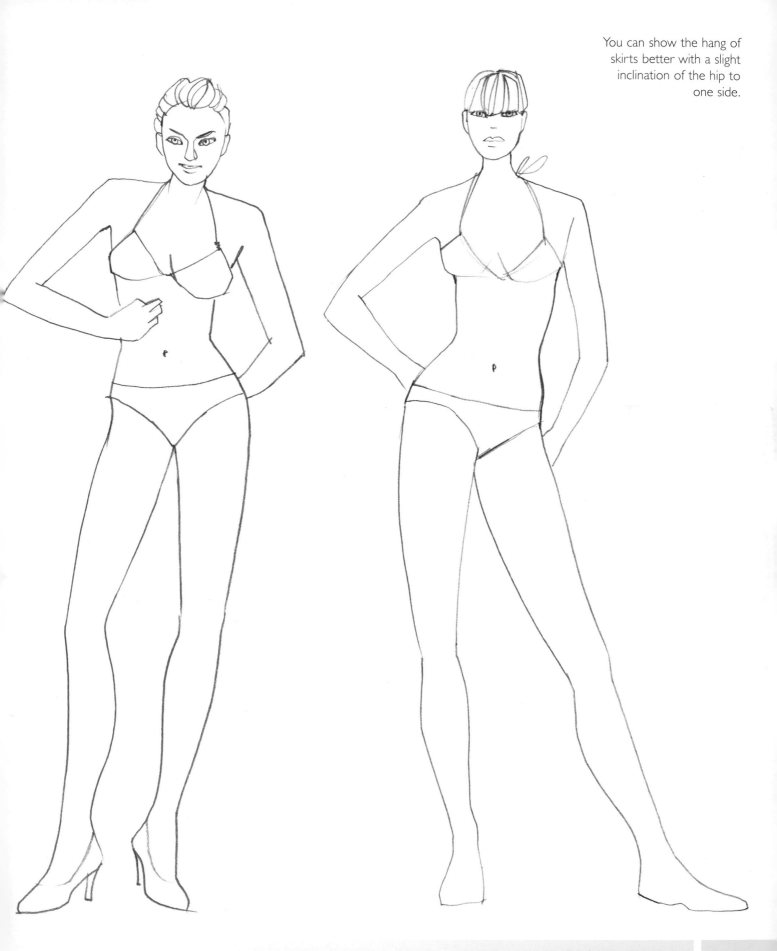

You can show the hang of skirts better with a slight inclination of the hip to one side.

Drawing the fashion sketch
with arms crossed allows
you to emphasize the
necklines of garments,
particularly those tied at
the neck such as halter tops.

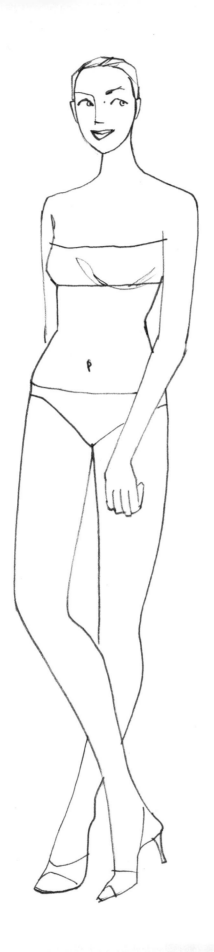

Arms falling to the sides emphasize strapless necklines and hands on the hips highlight closely fitting clothes.

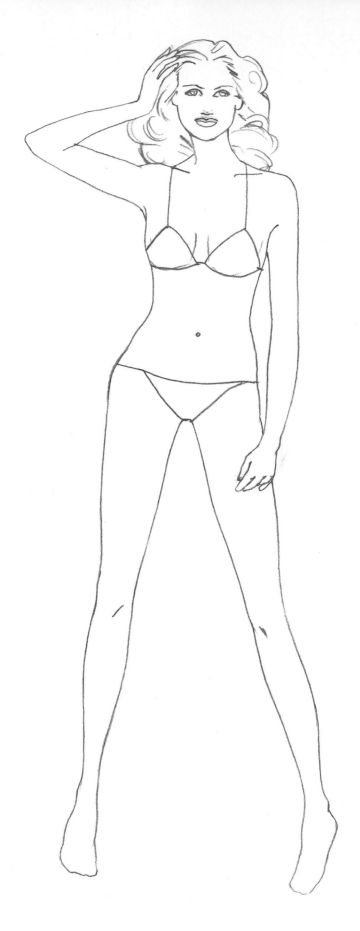

Raising the arms makes it
possible to focus more on the
clothes designed. Semi-profiles
are very useful for highlighting
the details of the design.

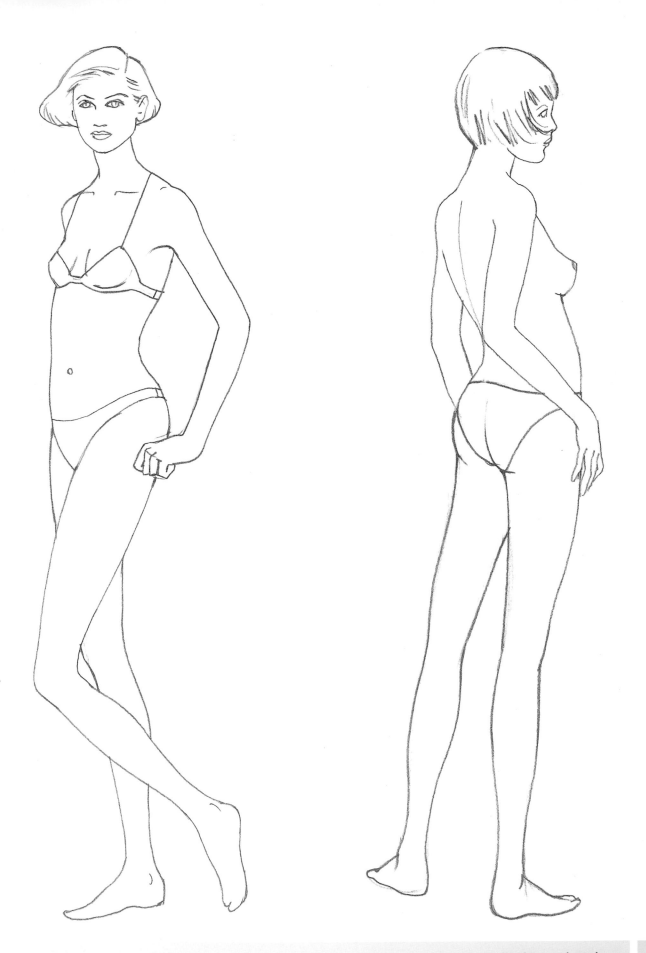

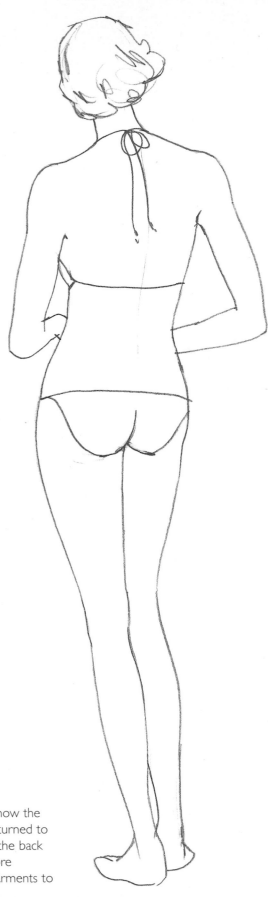

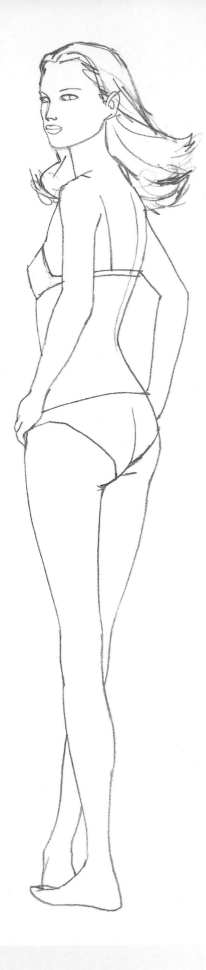

Sketches that show the whole back or turned to one side allow the back necklines of more sophisticated garments to be shown.

The weight falls on one of the legs while the other is seen in profile. This is a good pose for showing pants.

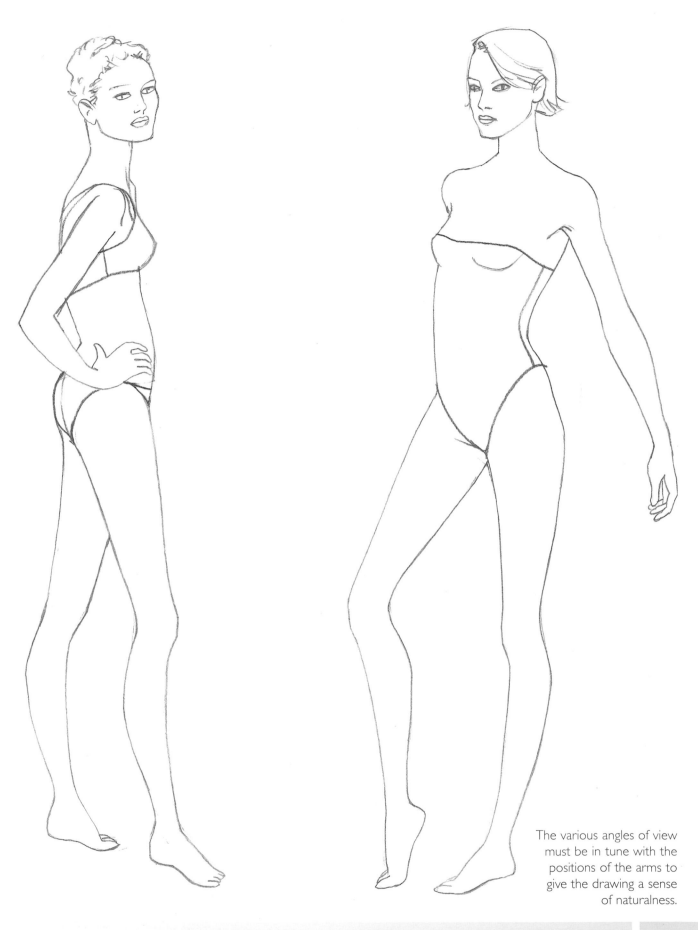

The various angles of view must be in tune with the positions of the arms to give the drawing a sense of naturalness.

Fashion Illustration: Figure Drawing

The back can to be shown fully or partially. When the body weight falls on one of the legs, the inclination of the shoulders will be opposite to that of the hips.

Fashion Illustration: Figure Drawing

You can play with the position of the legs to emphasize the characteristics of the various garments. The more the weight falls on just one leg, the closer this must be to the central axis of the sketch.

Crossing the legs involves a displacement of the body weight and the inclination of the hips. When showing a back neckline, to convey a certain sensuality the head is turned and the shoulders lean to one side.

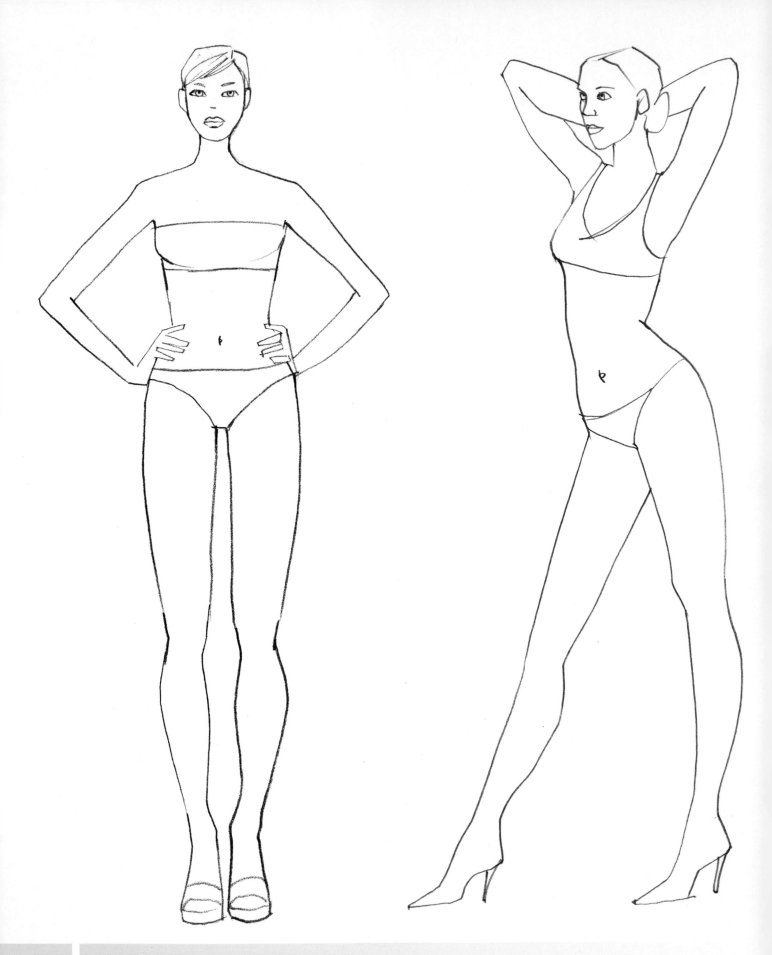

Fashion Illustration: Figure Drawing

The positioning of the arms makes it possible to show clothing in a more attractive way. By raising them to the level of the head, for example, the figure is stylized, achieving a perfect fashion sketch for drawing a dress. It is essential to find the point of support for the body when introducing other elements into illustrations.

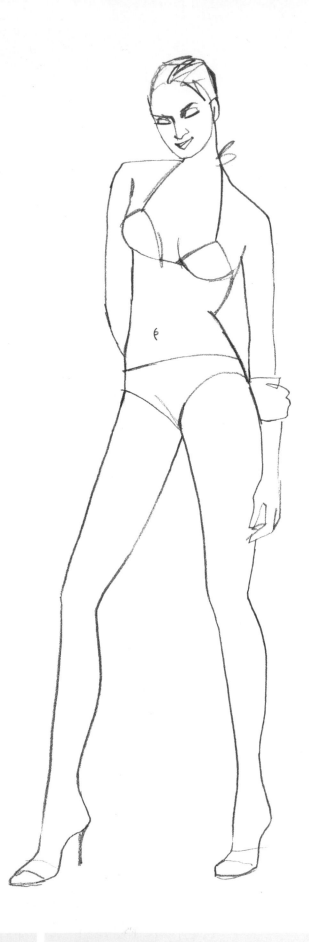
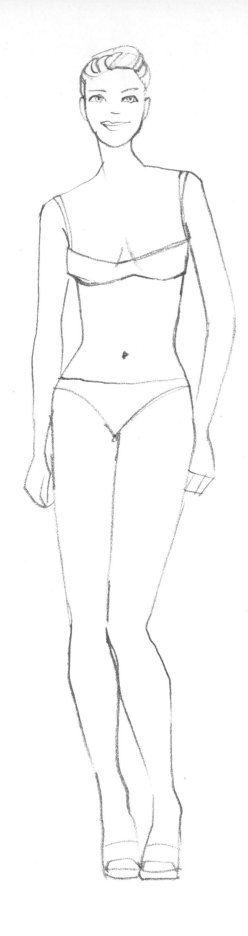

Fashion Illustration: Figure Drawing

When you want to show an inclination in the body, you must take into account that if the hip is lowered to one side then the shoulder must be raised. To design a strapless neckline we can opt to move the arms away from the trunk, raising them to shoulder level.

Following page
Half turns of the body and moving the legs apart are very useful devices when designing skirts, particularly long ones and those with delicate fabrics, which hang enveloping and highlighting the silhouette.

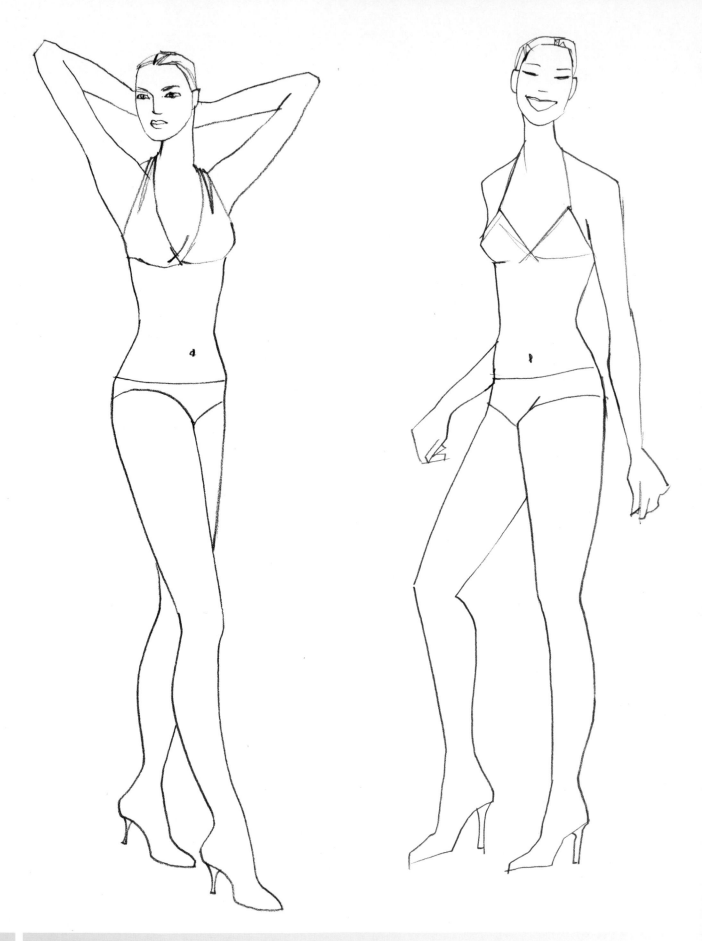

Fashion Illustration: Figure Drawing

Model in standing position

Fashion Illustration: Figure Drawing

Fashion Illustration: Figure Drawing

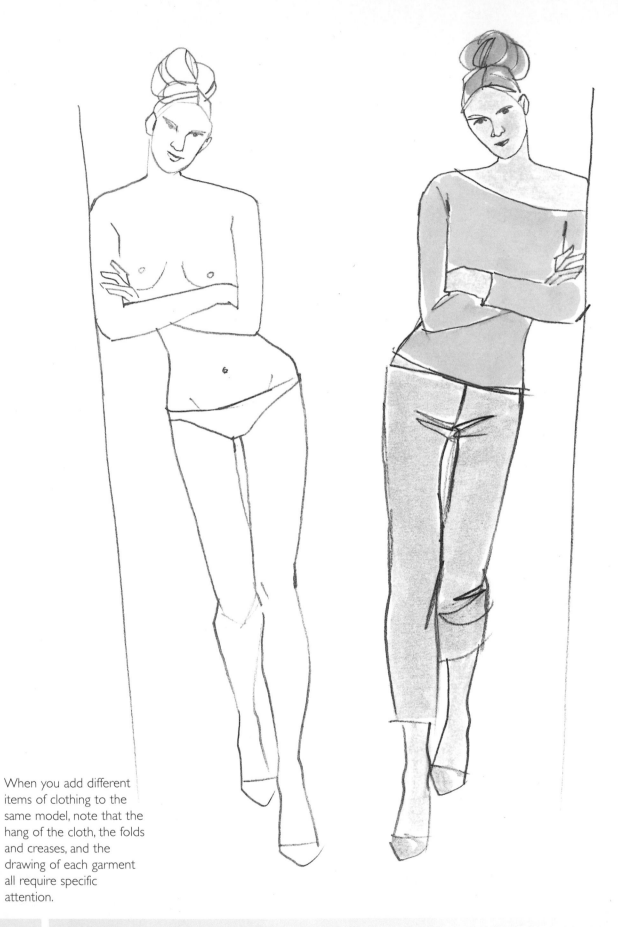

When you add different items of clothing to the same model, note that the hang of the cloth, the folds and creases, and the drawing of each garment all require specific attention.

Fashion Illustration: Figure Drawing

Watercolors are one of the most practical and appropriate techniques for giving fashion illustrations color.

Fashion Illustration: Figure Drawing

The sensuality of this pose
makes it very appropriate
for illustrating evening
gowns and dresses: both
very sophisticated
garments and elegant and
distinctive ensembles.

Playing with movement
not only offers variety, it
can also provide much
more information on the
garment. In this case, the
delicate hang of this
diaphanous dress becomes
more evident by raising
one of the arms.

From the innocence and delicateness of the pink dress you can move onto a genuine 1960s revival and even to a more formal, modern ensemble, all without needing to change the sketch.

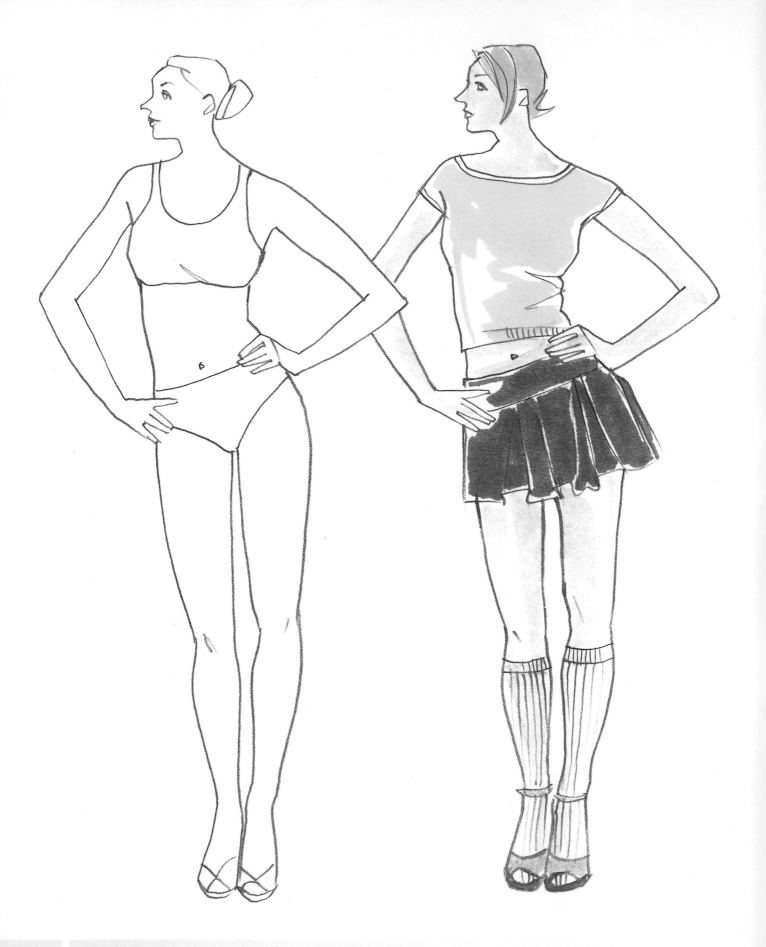

Fashion Illustration: Figure Drawing

By inclining the hips slightly you give movement to the design and the clothes fit the shape of the body's outline. The hands on the hips emphasize this inclination.

Fashion Illustration: Figure Drawing

You need to pay attention to the perspective in fashion sketches shown in profile. To include accessories, you can play with the positioning of the arms, attempting to separate them from the body to give a clearer view.

Cloths such as crêpe or tulle sit on the shoulders and hang delicately over the body. You can achieve the desired effect for these sensual transparencies with simple lines and a few brushstrokes of watercolor.

You can achieve a very feminine sketch for more flamboyant garments or dresses by giving movement to the legs and inclining the hips and shoulders.

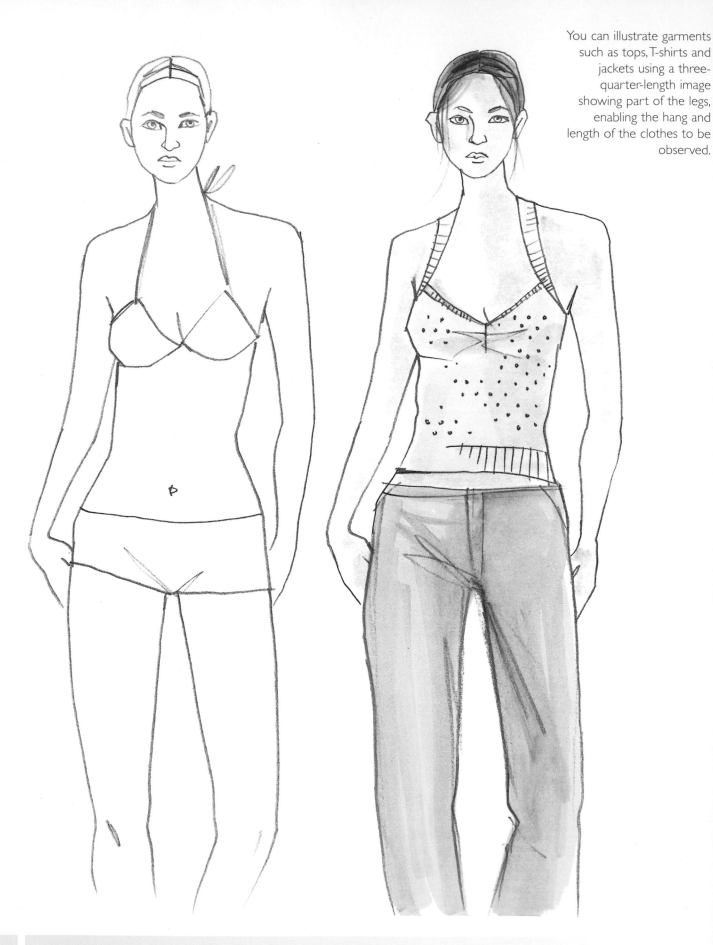

You can illustrate garments such as tops, T-shirts and jackets using a three-quarter-length image showing part of the legs, enabling the hang and length of the clothes to be observed.

Simpler, more static fashion sketches are the most suitable for unusual garments or those with mixed prints, because this type of clothing already attracts sufficient attention in its own right.

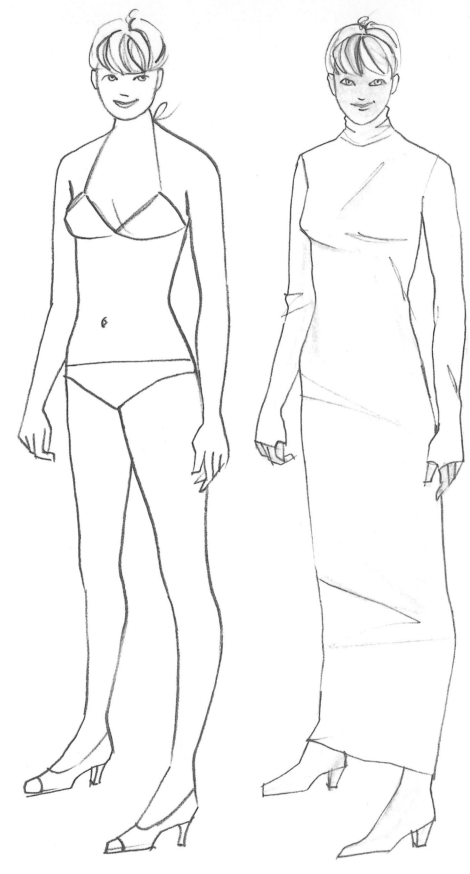

Fashion Illustration: Figure Drawing

Combinations of black and white are never out of fashion and are a very useful and simple resource when designing.

More daring poses help highlight items and specific aspects of the clothing, such as a low or strapless neckline or a top with a large bow.

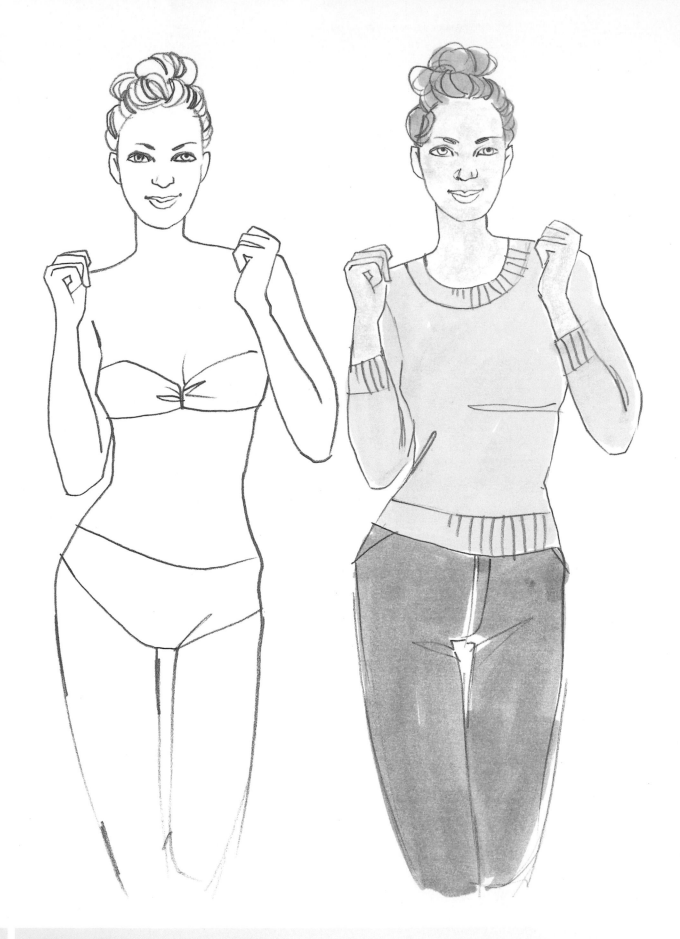

Fashion Illustration: Figure Drawing

Frontal representations are very appropriate for showing the collars of garments, both simple ones (flat, round) and more complex ones (with bows or shirt type).

Once you have completed the sketch, add the clothing and complete with the hairstyle and the accessories that are appropriate to the style you wish to create.

Fashion Illustration: Figure Drawing

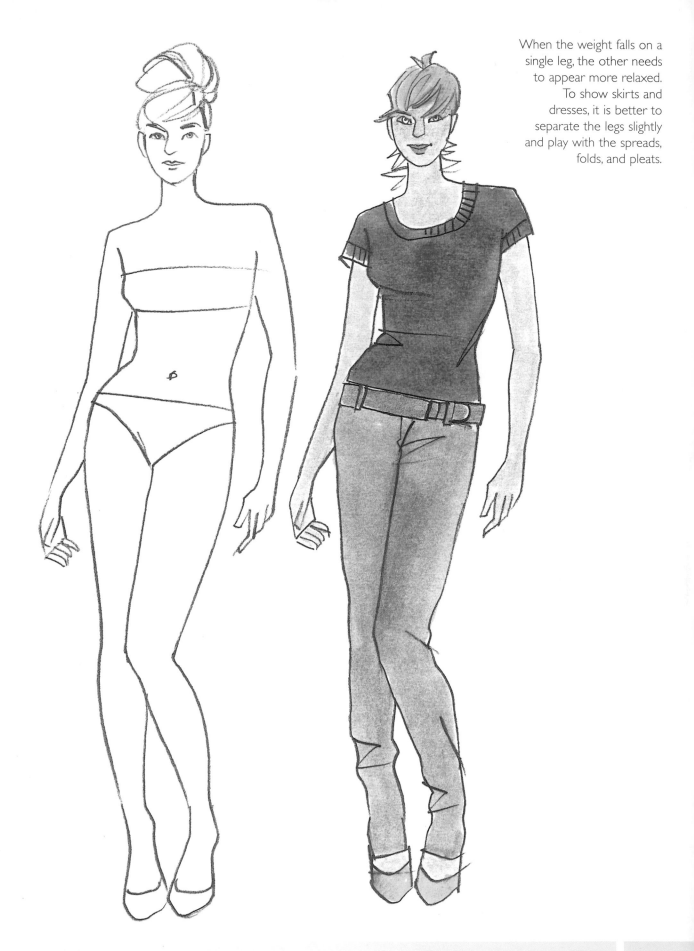

When the weight falls on a single leg, the other needs to appear more relaxed. To show skirts and dresses, it is better to separate the legs slightly and play with the spreads, folds, and pleats.

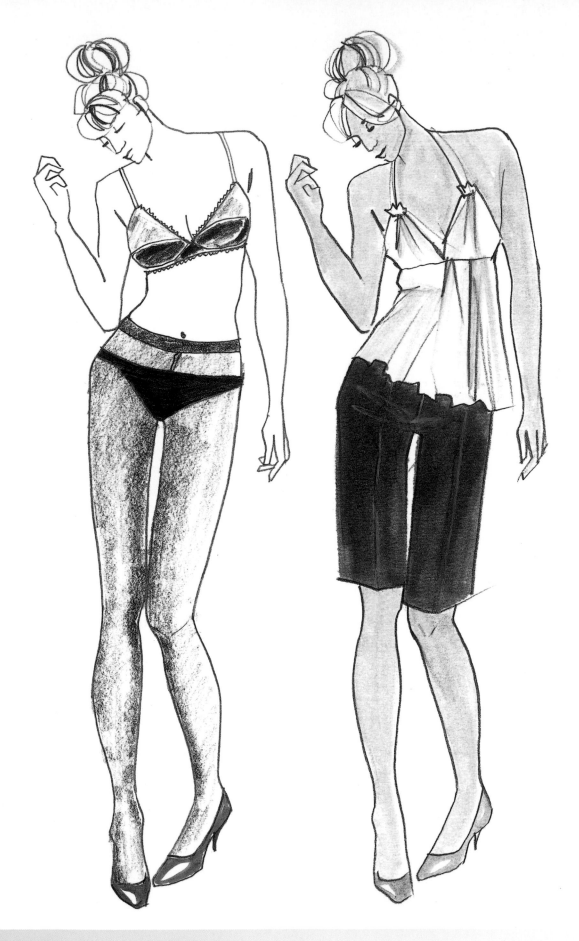

Fashion Illustration: Figure Drawing

By sloping the shoulders and positioning the arms carefully you can represent attitudes that, in combination with the clothes, achieve a more clear-cut style.

Fashion Illustration: Figure Drawing

The frontal drawing enables the tie at the neck of this dress to be seen in more detail, and the profile drawing shows the turtleneck of the sweater more clearly.

The elegance of the clothes shown in these illustrations is transmitted through the poses and expressions of the fashion sketches.

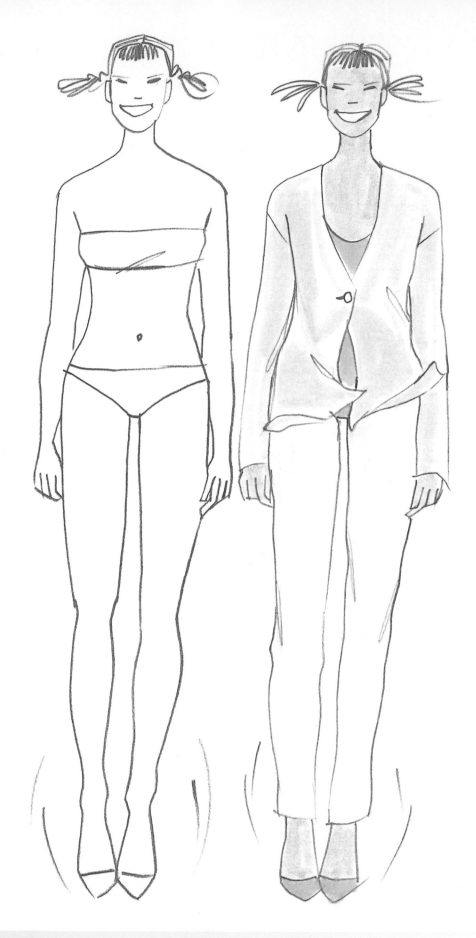

By representing movement you can give a sense of fullness to garments, as in the case of the jacket, or give the sketches a sense of dynamism.

Fashion Illustration: Figure Drawing

Illustrations with a more carefree feel are the most suitable for the more youthful, daring garments and combinations of both.

Fashion Illustration: Figure Drawing

Fashion Illustration: Figure Drawing

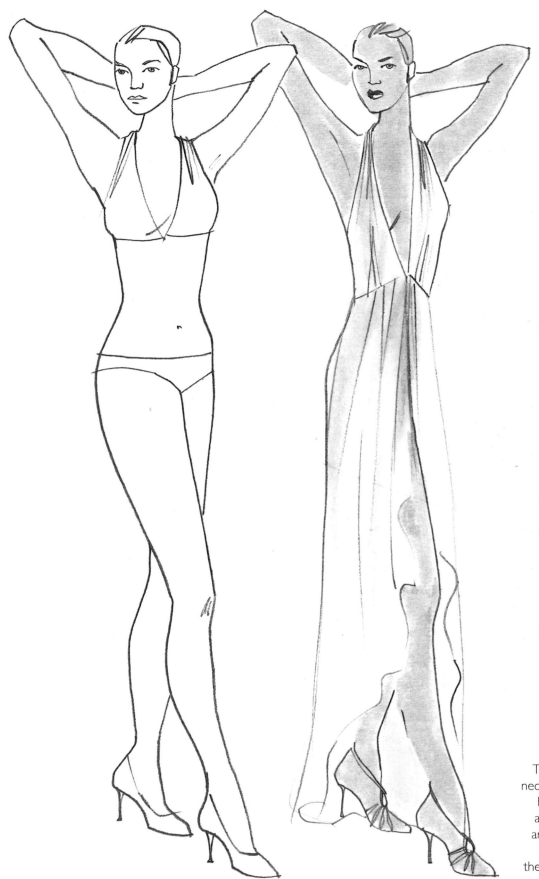

The sensuality of the neckline is accentuated by moving the arms away from the chest area, either by raising them or by placing them behind the back.

As well as allowing
the clothes to be seen
better, some poses and
accessories suggest a
certain attitude.

Fashion Illustration: Figure Drawing

Model in sitting position

When sketching a figure semi-seated, allowing the weight of the body to fall on a supporting point, you must pay special attention to the feet, which should appear more relaxed.

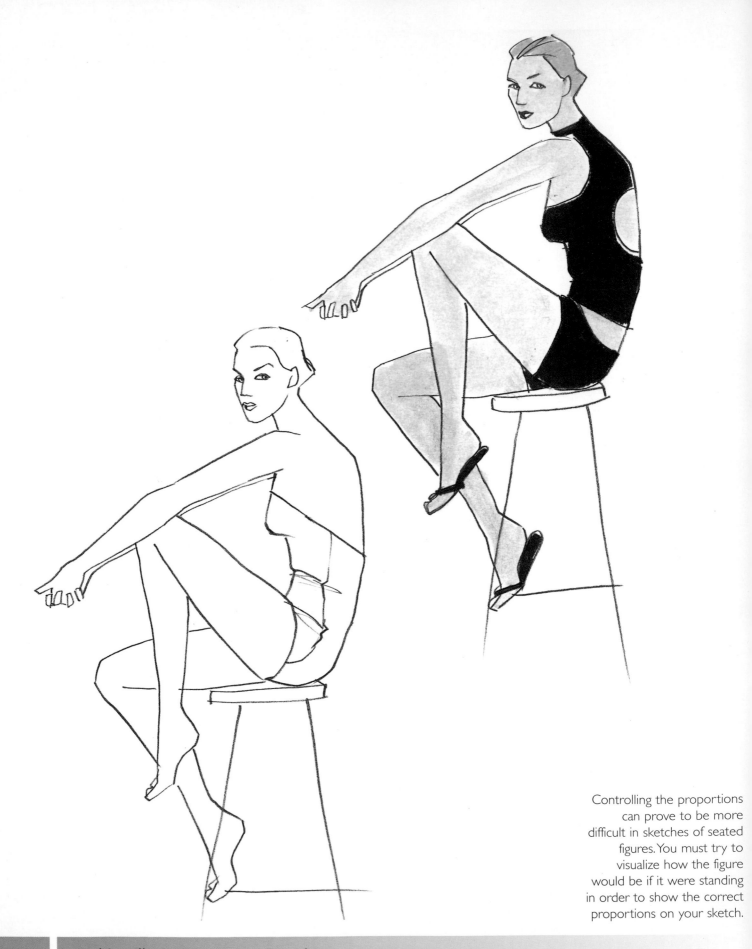

Controlling the proportions
can prove to be more
difficult in sketches of seated
figures. You must try to
visualize how the figure
would be if it were standing
in order to show the correct
proportions on your sketch.

This type of drawing
makes it possible to
introduce more variety
into the fashion illustration,
at the same time paying
attention to the curvature
of the back.

When crossing the legs and arms, keep in mind that the points of support multiply. Some rest on others and they must be proportionate.

This posture transmits a great deal of elegance and security; it is therefore very appropriate for attractive dresses and evening wear.

When sketched resting on the sofa, the body must adapt to its shape and appear much more relaxed.

Fashion Illustration: Figure Drawing

In these illustrations the forms of the collar, sleeves, and necklines are shown in profile.

Model in sitting position

Using seated poses with
more relaxed attitudes
allows you to sketch
models that are much
more youthful and
informal.

By showing the figure reclining on one side, this sketch expresses a great deal of sensuality and femininity.

Major fashion design schools

Europe

Belgium
LA CAMBRE
21 Abbaye de la Cambre
1000 Brussels, Belgium
T: + 32 2 626 17 80
www.lacambre.be

France
LISAA: ÉCOLE SUPÉRIEURE DES ARTS
APPLIQUÉS
13 Rue Vauquelin
75005 Paris, France
T: + 33 01 47 07 17 07
www.lisaa.com

STUDIO BERÇOT
T: + 33 01 42 46 15 55
studio.bercot@club-internet.fr
www.studio-bercot.com

Germany
ESMOD BERLIN
Schlesische Str. 29/30
Aufgang I & M
10997 Berlin, Germany
T: + 49 30 611 22 14
www.esmod.de

ESMOD MUNICH
Fraunhofer Str. 23h
80469 Munich, Germany
T: + 49 89 201 45 25
www.esmod.de

Italy
ACCADEMIA ITALIANA
Piazza Pitti 15
50125 Florence, Italy
T: + 39 055 284616
www.accademiaitaliana.com

A.R. STUDIO MILAN FASHION CAMPUS
Via Broggi 7
20129 Milan, Italy
T: + 39 02 268 22730
www.fashioncampus.it

ISTITUTO MARANGONI
Via Verri 4
20121 Milan, Italy
T: + 39 02 7631 6680
www.istitutomarangoni.com

ISTITUTO DI MODA BURGO
Piazza San Babila 5
20122 Milan, Italy
T: + 39 0278 3753
www.imb.it

POLIMODA INSTITUTE OF FASHION
DESIGN & MARKETING
Via Pisana 77
51043 Florence, Italy
T: + 39 055 739961
www.polimoda.com

UP TO DATE ACADEMY
Corso Vittorio Emanuele II 15
20122 Milan, Italy
T: + 39 02 76 26 791
www.fashionuptodate.com

Spain
ESDI
Av. Marquès de Comillas 79–83
08202 Sabadell, Barcelona, Spain
T: + 34 93 727 48 19
www.esdi.es

United Kingdom
CENTRAL SAINT MARTINS COLLEGE
OF ART & DESIGN
Catton Street, Holborn
London WCI, United Kingdom
T: + 44 (0) 20 7514 7027
www.csm.arts.ac.uk

LONDON CENTRE FOR FASHION
STUDIES
Bradley Close, White Lion Street
Islington, London N1 9PF, United Kingdom
T: + 44 (0) 20 7713 1991
www.fashionstudies.com

LONDON COLLEGE OF FASHION
20 John Princes Street
London W1G 0BJ, United Kingdom
T: + 44 (0) 20 7514 7407
www.fashion.arts.ac.uk

ROYAL COLLEGE OF ART
Kensington Gore
London SW7 2EU, United Kingdom
T: + 44 (0) 20 7590 4444
www.rca.ac.uk

THE ARTS INSTITUTE AT
BOURNEMOUTH
Wallisdown, Poole
Dorset BH12 5HH, United Kingdom
T: + 44 (0) 1202 533011
www.aib.ac.uk

UNIVERSITY COLLEGE FOR THE
CREATIVE ARTS
New Dover Road
Canterbury, Kent CT1 3AN, United
Kingdom
T: + 44 (0) 1227 817302
www.ucreasive.ac.uk

Africa and Oceania

South Africa
ELIZABETH GALLOWAY FASHION
DESIGN ACADEMY
26 Techno Park
Stellenbosch
7600 Western Cape, South Africa
T: + 27 (021) 88 00 77 5
www.safashionacademy.com

Australia
ELISABETH BENCE SCHOOL OF
FASHION
Level 2, 793–795 Pacific Highway
Gordon, NSW 2072, Australia
T: + (02) 9498 7240
www.thefashionschool.com.au

WHITE HOUSE INSTITUTE OF DESIGN
Level 3, 55 Liverpool Street
Sydney, NSW 2000, Australia
T: + 61 2 9267 8799
www.whitehouse-design.ed.au

Asia

China
THE HONG KONG POLYTECHNIC
UNIVERSITY
Corea A, 1st Floor
Hung Hom, Kowloon
Hong Kong, China
T: + 852 2766 5454
www.sd.polyu.edu.hk

India
PEARL ACADEMY OF FASHION
A 21/13, Naraina Industrial Area, Phase II
New Delhi 110028, India
T: + 414 176 93-94
www.pearlacademy.com

Japan
BUNKA FASHION COLLEGE
3-22-1, Yoyogi, Shibuya-ku,
151-8522 Tokyo, Japan
T: + 81 (0) 3 3299 2202
www.bunka-fc.ac.jp

North America

ACADEMY OF ART UNIVERSITY
79 New Montgomery Street, 4th Floor
San Francisco, CA 94105-3410, USA
T: + 415 274 2208
www.academyart.edu

AMERICAN INTERCONTINENTAL
UNIVERSITY
6600 Peachtree-Dunwoody Road
500 Embassy Road
Atlanta, GA 30328, USA
www.aiuniv.edu

BAUDER COLLEGE
384 Northyards Boulevard, NW
Suites 190 and 400
Atlanta, Georgia 30313, USA
T: + 800 241 3797
www.bauder.edu

BROOKS COLLEGE, LONG BEACH
4825 E. Pacific Coast Highway
Long Beach, CA 90804, USA
T: + 888 304 9777
www.brookscollege.edu

CALIFORNIA DESIGN COLLEGE
3440 Wilshire Blvd., 10th Floor
Los Angeles, CA 90010, USA
T: + 213 251 3636
www.artinstitutes.edu

FIDM
1010 Second Avenue
San Diego, CA 92101-4903, USA
T: + 619 235 2049
www.fidm.com

INTERNATIONAL ACADEMY OF
DESIGN & TECHNOLOGY – CHICAGO
One North State Street, Suite 500
Chicago, IL 60602, USA
www.iadtchicago.edu

PARIS FASHION INSTITUTE
355 West Fourth St.
Boston, MA 02127, USA
T: + 617 268 0026
www.parisfashion.org

PARSONS: THE NEW STYLE FOR
DESIGN
65 5th Ave. Ground Floor
New York, NY 10003, USA
T: + 1 212 229 8989
www.parsons.edu

PRATT INSTITUTE: FASHION DESIGN
144 West 14th Street
New York, NY 10011, USA
T: + 1 212 718 789 1105
www.pratt.edu

WESTWOOD COLLEGE
7350 N. Broadway
Denver, CO 80221, USA
awarden@westwood.edu
www.westwoodcollege.com